D1573247

THE
CREATION
of THE
U.S. CONSTITUTION

A HISTORY PERSPECTIVES BOOK

Roberta Baxter

Published in the United States of America
by Cherry Lake Publishing
Ann Arbor, Michigan
www.cherrylakepublishing.com

Consultants: Betsy Glade, Assistant Professor, Department of History, St. Cloud State
University; Marla Conn, ReadAbility, Inc.
Editorial direction: Red Line Editorial
Book design: Sleeping Bear Press

Photo Credits: Library of Congress, cover, 24, 26; Public Domain, cover, 14; Henry
Singleton, 4; John Serz/Library of Congress, 5; William Bradford/Library of Congress, 7;
Gilbert Stuart/Library of Congress, 11; Albert Rosenthal/Library of Congress, 15;
W.J. Bennett, G. Cooke/Library of Congress, 17; Currier & Ives/Library of Congress, 20;
North Wind/North Wind Picture Archives, 22; John Chester Buttre and Ezra Ames/
Library of Congress, 28; Bettmann/Corbis, 30

Library of Congress Cataloging-in-Publication Data
Baxter, Roberta, 1952-
  The creation of the US Constitution / Roberta Baxter.
     pages cm. -- (Perspectives library)
  Includes index.
   ISBN 978-1-63137-616-0 (hardcover) -- ISBN 978-1-63137-661-0 (pbk.)
-- ISBN 978-1-63137-706-8 (pdf ebook) -- ISBN 978-1-63137-751-8 (hosted ebook)
1. United States. Constitution--Juvenile literature. 2. Constitutional history--
United States--Juvenile literature. I. Title. II. Title: Creation of the United States
Constitution.
E303.B39 2014
342.7302'9--dc23

                         2014004582

Cherry Lake Publishing would like to acknowledge the work of
The Partnership for 21st Century Skills. Please visit *www.p21.org*
for more information.

Printed in the United States of America
Corporate Graphics Inc.
July 2014

TABLE OF CONTENTS

In this book, you will read about the creation of the U.S. Constitution from three perspectives. There was much debate over the U.S. Constitution. Some wanted a strong national government, while others feared losing state control. As you'll see, the same event can look different depending on one's point of view.

1

Mercy Pages
Serving Girl

It is 1787—an exciting time to be working at Mrs. House's **boardinghouse**. I see important men such as Benjamin Franklin, George Washington, and Alexander Hamilton in the streets of Philadelphia. Every day they meet at the State House.

Here at Mrs. House's, we have James Madison of Virginia as one of our boarders. He is a

quiet man, but I like him. He always thanks me
when I bring him food at the table or water for his
room. His room has stacks of books that he brought
with him. My fingers itch to open and read them.

▲ *The State House in Philadelphia, Pennsylvania, was the site of the
Constitutional **Convention** in 1787.*

One day Mr. Madison asked me where I was from. I told him I lived on my family's farm a few miles from Philadelphia until my father died in an accident. Forgetting my place as a servant, I told him how good it was that the Articles of **Confederation** would be changed. He looked at me in surprise and then asked, "How do you know about such things?" I told him my father had always been interested in how our country was governed. He often read what newspapers he could find and we discussed the news.

My father thought that the states were too loosely connected. They did not always work together to protect the country. Congress couldn't require taxes from states or control business between states. Father said that the central government under the Articles of Confederation was too weak. The states act like separate countries rather than part of the United States.

The TIMES are Dreadful, Dismal, Doleful, Dolorous, and DOLLAR-LESS.

NUMB. 1195.

Thursday, *October* 31, 1765.

THE

PENNSYLVANIA JOURNAL;

AND

WEEKLY ADVERTISER.

EXPIRING: In Hopes of a Resurrection to LIFE again.

I AM sorry to be obliged to acquaint my Readers, that as The STAMP-ACT, is fear'd to be obligatory upon us after the *First of November* ensuing, (the *fatal To morrow*) the Publisher of this Paper unable to bear the Burthen, has thought it expedient TO STOP awhile, in order to deliberate, whether any Methods can be found to elude the Chains forged for us, and escape the insupportable Slavery, which it is hoped, from the last Representations now made against that Act, may be effected. Mean while, I must earnestly Request every Individual of my Subscribers, many of whom have been long behind Hand, that they would immediately Discharge their respective Arrears that I may be able, not only to support myself during the Interval, but be better prepared to proceed again with this Paper, whenever an opening for that Purpose appears, which I hope will be soon.

WILLIAM BRADFORD

▲ *Political news was often spread through different journals and newspapers, such as the* Pennsylvania Journal.

Mr. Madison said that I could read his newspapers after he finished them. I was amazed by his kindness.

At the end of May, a convention began at the State House. One of the newspapers explained the meeting was for the sole purpose of revising the Articles of Confederation. My father would have been happy with that news.

I walked by the State House on my way to the market one day. I saw that dirt was put over the cobblestones on the street. A young boy told me that it was done to quiet the street noise so that the men inside could better think and speak. A guard stands at the door of the State House, so no one is allowed in except the **delegates**. The men need secrecy

THINK ABOUT IT

▶ Determine the main point of this chapter. Pick out one piece of evidence that supports it.

so they can discuss their opinions freely without risk of their ideas being reported in the newspapers. I wish all the people could know what is happening and be able to share our opinions. But I can understand that the delegates want to work it out between themselves first. All the windows are closed, so I know it must be hot and uncomfortable inside.

Every day Mr. Madison looks more and more tired. I can tell that the heat in that closed room bothers him. Still, he writes his papers way into the night.

On September 17, 1787, a new Constitution of the United States was signed at the Constitutional Convention. Now it will go to each state for approval.

Mr. Madison has left and I continue working at the boardinghouse. I collect newspapers after

SECOND SOURCE

▶ Find a second source about the Publius articles, which were later known as *The Federalist* papers. Compare that source with the one here.

our guests have read them. Long articles from an anonymous person known as Publius started to appear in the newspapers. The articles encourage people to support the new Constitution. Publius writes that our central government was weak. The author supports a strong central government. He writes that the power of the central government would not take away from the power of the states.

Some people believe that Mr. Madison is one of the writers of the articles by Publius. Each article is numbered. Number 14 is about what my father would have feared—that foreign nations might think we are weak and attack. If the states don't work together to protect the whole country, another country might try to invade. The United States must stick together to be safe from attack.

JAMES MADISON.
FOURTH PRESIDENT OF THE UNITED STATES.

From the Original Series painted by Stuart
for the late L. Leopott of Boston

▲ *James Madison was later elected the fourth president of the United States.*

ARTICLES OF CONFEDERATION

The Articles of Confederation loosely joined the different states under a weak central government. Each state's government held most of the power. The U.S. Constitution replaced the Articles of Confederation. The Constitution placed most of the power with the national government.

Other newspaper articles state that the Constitution may not protect the rights of citizens. Some say they will not **ratify** the Constitution without a Bill of Rights defining the basic rights of all citizens. Others argue that a list of rights is not necessary in the Constitution. I'm not sure what I think.

By June 1788, 9 of 13 states had ratified the Constitution. It is now approved. Pennsylvania, my state, was the second one to ratify the Constitution.

Our new government takes power in March 1789. Congress will work on a Bill of Rights as was promised when the Constitution was approved. It is a proud time with a new government for the United States.

William Barton

Law Clerk

In early 1787, I was chosen to serve as a law clerk to Mr. Patrick Henry in Prince Edward County, Virginia. Mr. Henry served in our legislature and as the governor of Virginia during the Revolutionary War and after. Now he has a thriving law practice.

Sadness has struck his family in recent years. His brother-in-law was killed fighting Indians in Kentucky. Mr. Henry grieved that this occurred because our Congress does not have the funds to provide a defense for our frontier. Congress does not have the power to tax the states, so it can't raise money. States are supposed to send support to the central government, but they often don't.

Mr. Henry explained to me that he thought the central government should have limited power to tax states. Then John Jay of New York changed Mr. Henry's mind. Mr. Jay was in charge

John Jay served as the first chief justice of the U.S. Supreme Court beginning in 1789. ▶

of the country's foreign affairs. He was working on a **treaty** with Spain. He proposed to limit U.S. use of the Mississippi River for 25 years if Spain would open ports in its country for U.S. ships. Mr. Jay went outside of his instructions from Congress. That kind of treaty would hurt the state of Virginia. Our western farmers need the Mississippi to ship their products. If they could not sell their crops, they could not make money and many of them would lose their farms. Mr. Henry was angered by Mr. Jay's discussions with Spain. Luckily Congress did not pass the treaty, so the crisis passed. But the incident made Mr. Henry suspicious of officials going beyond their powers and hurting the country.

Mr. Henry received a letter from our governor today. The governor wants Mr. Henry to be a delegate at the convention to revise the Articles of Confederation. Governor Randolph wrote that our country faces danger because of the weakness of our government. Mr. Henry refused to go though. I asked him why. He said that if an official from a weak government could propose a treaty that could damage our state, a strong central government could hurt us more. He believes that Virginia, being the richest state with the most people, could make agreements with other states on its own. A strong national government and a strong president could just be another type of **tyranny** similar to the control Great Britain had over the colonies. So Mr. Henry closely follows what happens at the convention.

He believes that the Articles of Confederation should be changed, but he fears a stronger central government would take away the rights of states and citizens.

Richmond, Virginia, was a thriving U.S. city in the late 1700s. ▶

We heard little about the convention in Philadelphia through the summer. The newspapers reported that the delegates have taken an oath of silence. I was skeptical of that idea because in a **republic**, all should have their say.

Finally, the delegates have signed an entirely new Constitution. We received a copy of the document. It starts out by declaring that the people want to form a more perfect union. I wonder if it will happen.

Soon after, Mr. Henry got a letter from George Washington. Mr. Washington wants the Constitution to be adopted by the states. He fears that our country is in danger and that **anarchy** could come without a strong central government. Mr. Henry wrote back that he was not in favor of this Constitution and felt great concern about our

THINK ABOUT IT

▶ Determine the main point of this chapter. What facts support the main point? Are any surprising to you?

country. The Virginia convention to debate signing the U.S. Constitution meets in June 1788. Mr. Henry will be a delegate.

For the last year, we have read articles in newspapers between those in favor of the Constitution, known as the Federalists, and those like Mr. Henry who oppose it. Those against the Constitution are the Anti-Federalists.

We also heard about the conventions in other states. By January 1788, five states voted to ratify the Constitution. Massachusetts had a long battle between the two sides before its approval. The state added that it wanted a Bill of Rights included in the Constitution.

Once the Virginia convention began, Mr. Henry argued against the new Constitution. He said that

ANALYZE THIS

► Analyze two of the accounts in this book of the creation of the U.S. Constitution. How are they different? How are they the same?

it brought about a change as big as the Revolutionary War, which freed us from Great Britain. In one speech, he spoke for seven hours.

I heard part of another speech. Mr. Henry argued that the Constitution took away rights that had been given to Virginia's citizens by its state constitution. He argued that our rights would be given up to Congress

"GIVE ME LIBERTY, OR GIVE ME DEATH!"

▲ *Patrick Henry is known for his famous speeches, including one given to the Virginia assembly in 1775 before the Revolutionary War.*

unless a Bill of Rights was added to the Constitution. He insisted that all citizens should have freedom of speech and the press and the right to a trial by jury. None of those rights are defined in the new Constitution. Mr. Madison said that he would push for a Bill of Rights as the first **amendment** to the Constitution.

When the vote was taken, Virginia ratified the new Constitution by a vote of 89 to 79. I pray that the new government will be fair for all our citizens.

THE BILL OF RIGHTS

James Madison kept his promise to work for a Bill of Rights. On September 25, 1789, Congress passed 12 amendments. These amendments were sent to the states for approval. Ten of the amendments passed. They became the Bill of Rights. They define the basic rights of all citizens of the United States.

Robert Moore

Apprentice Printer

My work as an apprentice printer in New York City began in the early summer of 1787. One of the newspapers that our shop prints is the *Independent Journal.* All summer I learned to place tiny metal blocks of letters to make words and prepare the press with the proper amount of ink. I also read and published articles about the convention meeting in Philadelphia.

Little news came from the delegates because they did not allow reporters into the sessions. I am concerned that if changes are made to create a strong central government, power will be taken away from the states and people. I will wait and see what those men in Philadelphia propose and then make up my mind.

Finally, we know what the convention has written—a new Constitution. It was printed in our newspaper. I proofread every word before it was published. It is a stirring document. Now the states need to debate and vote whether to ratify the Constitution.

On October 27, 1787, the newspaper published the first of a series of articles supporting the Constitution. The anonymous author, who signed his name as

SECOND SOURCE

▶ Find a second source about the creation of the U.S. Constitution. Compare it to Robert Moore's account.

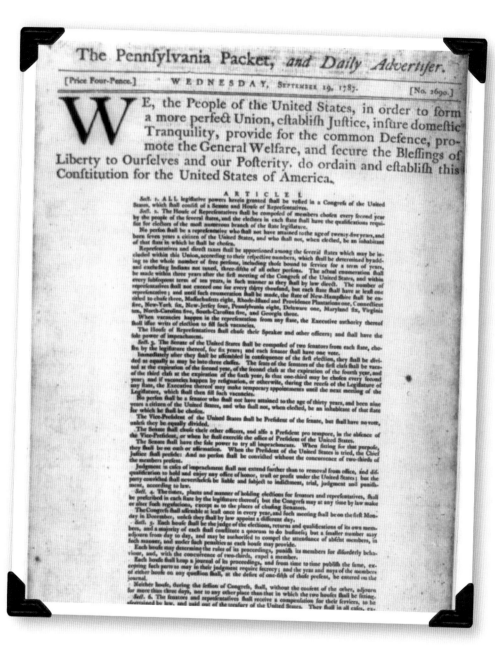

▲ *The U.S. Constitution was printed in newspapers, including* The Pennsylvania Packet.

Publius, said that we are called to decide on the new Constitution. He will show in future articles that we need a strong central government, which will lead to liberty and strength.

THE FEDERALIST PAPERS

In papers found after Alexander Hamilton's death, it was revealed that he wrote 51 of the Publius articles, which were later published as a book called *The Federalist*. James Madison wrote 29 articles and John Jay wrote five. Thomas Jefferson called *The Federalist* papers the best lessons on government ever written. The articles have become an important source explaining the original goals of the U.S. Constitution.

We published many more of the articles. The authors are unknown, but many think John Jay, Alexander Hamilton, and James Madison wrote them. I have seen Hamilton and Madison walking together on the street. Mr. Madison is a delegate to the Congress that meets in New York under the present laws. Mr. Hamilton is often dressed in bright colors, while Mr. Madison is always in black.

The newspaper also published articles from writers who are against the

THE

FEDERALIST:

A COLLECTION OF

E S S A Y S,

WRITTEN IN FAVOUR OF THE

NEW CONSTITUTION,

AS AGREED-UPON BY THE

FEDERAL CONVENTION,

SEPTEMBER 17, 1787.

IN TWO VOLUMES.
VOL. I.

NEW-YORK:
PRINTED AND SOLD BY JOHN TIEBOUT,
No. 358 PEARL-STREET.
1799.

◀ The Federalist *was first published as a book in 1788. It contained articles written in favor of the new U.S. Constitution.*

new Constitution. These Anti-Federalist writers fear that the government will become too powerful and will take away our rights. We fought the Revolutionary War to free ourselves from that kind of tyranny, and we will not allow it again.

I see good points on both sides of the argument. As delegates in each state debate the document, we hear more reasons for and against a new Constitution. Throughout the winter of 1787, six states, including Pennsylvania, voted to ratify the Constitution. In New York, the debate has been bitter. Governor George Clinton is chairman of the state's convention. He is strongly against the Constitution. Mr. Hamilton is a delegate and he argues for it.

We published articles against the Constitution by another anonymous author. He is known as Cato. He warns against strengthening the government. It might give power over the whole country to only a few men.

▲ *New York's first governor was George Clinton.*

Word came that a ninth state, New Hampshire, has ratified the Constitution. That is all the votes needed to approve the document.

The U.S. Constitution is now the basis of our government. Still Mr. Hamilton wants New York to ratify it to show support from our large state.

On June 25, Virginia ratified the Constitution. In our New York convention, delegates warned that there might be civil war. At a Fourth of July parade in Albany, people rioted over the Constitution and one person was killed.

Finally, on July 26, the New York convention ratified the U.S. Constitution. The Anti-Federalists demand that a Bill of Rights be added to protect the rights of citizens. The new national government will meet in New York in April 1789.

THINK ABOUT IT

▶ Examine the information about the Anti-Federalists. Does their point of view surprise you?

LOOK, LOOK AGAIN

Take a look at this image showing the signing of the U.S. Constitution. Answer the following questions:

1. How would a boardinghouse worker describe this scene to her friends? What might she notice?

2. How would an Anti-Federalist react to this image? What might he tell other citizens about the signing of the U.S. Constitution?

3. What would a Federalist, such as Robert Moore, think about this image? How might he describe this scene?

GLOSSARY

amendment (uh-MEND-muhnt) a change that is made to a law or legal document

anarchy (AN-ur-kee) a situation without order or a leader in control

boardinghouse (BOR-ding-houss) a house that provides food and lodging for paying guests

confederation (kuhn-fed-uh-RAY-shun) a union of people or groups acting together

convention (kuhn-VEN-shuhn) a large gathering of people who have a similar interest, such as a political issue

delegate (DEL-uh-gate) a person who represents others or an entity, such as a state, at a meeting

ratify (RAT-uh-fye) to approve or officially agree to something

republic (ri-PUHB-lik) a type of government in which a country's people elect representatives to govern the country

treaty (TREE-tee) an official agreement that is made between countries or groups

tyranny (TIHR-uh-nee) cruel or unjust rule of a country

LEARN MORE

Further Reading

Cheney, Lynne. *We the People: The Story of Our Constitution*. New York: Simon & Schuster Books for Young Readers, 2008.
Fritz, Jean. *Alexander Hamilton: The Outsider*. New York: G.P. Putnam's Sons, 2011.
Leavitt, Amie Jane. *The Constitution: Defender of Freedom*. Kennett Square, PA: Purple Toad Publishing, 2014.

Web Sites

Constitution
http://teachingamericanhistory.org/library/constitution/
This Web site has source documents related to the creation of the U.S. Constitution.

Constitution of the United States
http://www.archives.gov/exhibits/charters/constitution.html
This Web site includes the images of the preserved Constitution as well as articles about its creation.

INDEX

ABOUT THE AUTHOR

Roberta Baxter has written about history and science for students of all ages. Her latest history books include *The Bill of Rights, The Battle of Gettysburg,* and *The Dropping of the Atomic Bombs.* Baxter has always enjoyed reading about the founding of the United States.